Introduction to Letters and Sounds

This book will help your child learn the letters and sounds they need to know to read, spell and write. It contains:

- an introduction to synthetic phonics
- guidance on how to say the sounds
- activity pages
- a practice grid of 42 phonemes (sounds).

Synthetic phonics is all about sounds. In synthetic phonics children are taught 42 speech sounds, how to match sounds to letters and then how to use these skills for reading and spelling. You can learn more about synthetic phonics on page 3 of this book.

Using the pack

The pack contains a 45-minute DVD taken from the BBC TV programme, **Fun with Phonics.** The DVD introduces 42 sounds by presenting the easiest sounds first and ending with the most difficult sounds. They are:

- 26 alphabet sounds in groups
  s a t p i n m d g o c k/ck
  e u r h b f l j v w x y z qu

- 16 digraphs (sounds  two letters) ch sh t
  oa oo OO ue ar c

With your child, watch a clip introducing one sound, then try one or more of the relevant activity pages in this book. Don't cover more than two or three new sounds each time, although quickly revising sounds you've done before can be helpful.

Included in the pack is a colourful poster illustrating all 42 sounds as featured in the programmes.

Activities

Letter/sound match: these activity pages give your child practice in matching the sound to the letter. Look at the pictures together and ask your child to say the words. Then ask them to find the letter each word starts with from the ones at the top of the page. Be encouraging and praise them when they get it right.

Blending: once your child has learned enough sounds to make up a few simple words (the first group of sounds: s a t p i n), have a go at the blending activity sheets. Ask your child to say the sounds that make up each word on the page and blend them together to say the word. Then ask your child to point to the correct picture.

Letter/sound match (writing): if you think your child is ready, encourage your child to practise writing letters in the air. Once they can write one group of letters, ask them to write the correct start letter for the word on the line below each picture on these pages.

Starting writing

When your child starts writing, check that they are holding the pencil correctly. They should grip the pencil just above the painted edge between their index finger and thumb. Then they can flex this finger and thumb like frogs' legs. Next, they place the third finger behind the pencil, acting as a rest. Do the grip yourself to show your child. Children often like to say 'frogs' legs' as they grip the pencil, then 'frog on a log' as they put the third finger behind. Now they're ready to write.

About synthetic phonics

In synthetic phonics there are three essential tools for literacy:
- matching letter to sound (reading) and sound to letter (spelling)
- blending (sliding single sounds together to read an unfamiliar word)
- segmenting (hearing the individual sounds in words, and writing the letters down to spell a word).

Letter/sound match

First, your child starts to learn the individual sounds (phonemes). They will learn at least forty-two speech phonemes of the English language.

After learning to hear individual phonemes, your child sees them written down as a letter. The letters are described as 'the picture of the sound written down'. This applies both to the single alphabet letters where one sound is represented by one letter (for example, s, a, p); and to digraphs, or letter pairs, where one sound is represented by two letters (for example, sh, th).

Blending sounds into words

As soon as your child has learned four consonants (p, t, s, n) and two vowels (i and a), they can begin to blend (synthesize) these sounds together to read unfamiliar words. First they sound out the letters, then they say the word. If your child needs extra practice with learning how to blend, sound out the word yourself, sliding the sounds closely together so that your child can get the word. The list on page 4 of this book tells you how to pronounce the phonemes.

Segmenting words into sounds

For spelling and writing, your child needs to say a word, then break it down (segment it) into its individual phonemes and write them down. Your child can start practising this skill at the same time as they start blending (see above). It may help your child to remember the order of the sounds in the word if they tap once with their fingers on a table for each sound, then write the letters.

Saying the sounds

Here are the 42 main speech sounds your child will learn in synthetic phonics, with a guide to how to say them.

Letter names as we learn to say them in the alphabet are not stressed at this early stage of learning.

s **as in** sat	w **as in** wet
a **as in** ant	x **as in** box
t **as in** tin	y **as in** yet
p **as in** pen	z **as in** zip
i **as in** ink	qu **as in** queen
n **as in** net	ch **as in** chip
m **as in** man	sh **as in** shop
d **as in** dog	th **as in** this, moth
g **as in** gum	ng **as in** ring
o **as in** ox	ai **as in** rain
c **as in** cat	ee **as in** weep
k **as in** kit (ck **makes the**	ie **as in** tie
e **as in** egg **same sound)**	oa **as in** boat
u **as in** under	oo **as in** book
r **as in** rat	OO **as in** moon
h **as in** hen	ue **as in** cue
b **as in** bag	ar **as in** farm
f **as in** fan	or **as in** port
l **as in** log	er **as in** number
j **as in** jug	ou **as in** mouth
v **as in** van	oi **as in** coin

Say each word, then choose the correct letter for the start sound from the ones below.

s   a   t   p   i   n

The words are: tiger, net, snail, ink, ant, pen.

Say the sounds, work out the word and point to the correct picture.

pin		
tap		
pan		
tin		

Letter/sound match (writing) s a t p i n

Say each word and write the correct letter for the start sound from the ones below.

s a t p i n

The words are: tooth, net, sun, ink, ant, peg.

Say the sounds, work out the word and point to the correct picture.

nap		
sit		
nip		
sip		

Say each word, then choose the correct letter for the start sound from the ones below.

m   d   g   o   c   k/ck

The words are: cat, king, orange, goat, dog, man.

Say the sounds, work out the word and point to the correct picture.

cap		
mop		
dot		
kit		

Say each word and write the correct letter for the start sound from the ones below.

m　　d　　g　　o　　c　　k/ck

The words are: car, kid, girl, milk, orange, dolphin.

Say each word, then choose the correct letter for the start sound from the ones below.

e   u   r   h   b   f

The words are: elephant, frog, hook, umbrella, ring, bag.

Say the sounds, work out the word and point to the correct picture.

gum		
bug		
fan		
hat		

Say each word and write the correct letter for the start sound from the ones below.

e   u   r   h   b   f

The words are: bee, frog, elbow, umbrella, hen, rail.

Say the sounds, work out the word and point to the correct picture.

red		
bat		
fan		
nut		

Say each word, then choose the correct letter for the start sound from the ones below.

l   j   v   w

The words are: web, vet, leg, van, jet, wig.

Say the sounds, work out the word and point to the correct picture.

wig		
jet		
log		
vet		

Say each word and write the correct letter for the start sound from the ones below.

l   j   v   w

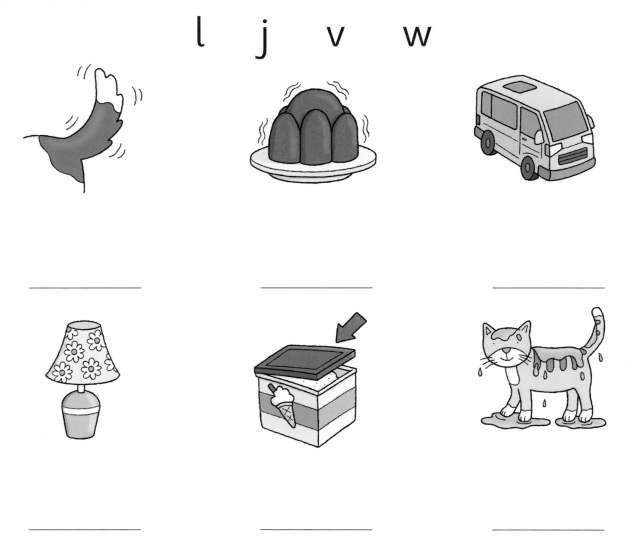

The words are: wag, jelly, van, lamp, lid, wet.

Say each word, then choose the correct letter/s for the start sound.
Choose the letter for the end sound of the last two pictures.

x   y   z   qu

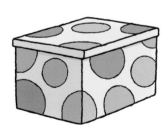

The words are: yell, zigzag, queen, quiz, box, fox.

Say the sounds, work out the word and point to the correct picture.

box		
zip		
yak		
quiz		

Say each word and write the correct letter/s for the start sound from the ones below. Write the end sound for the last picture.

x   y   z   qu

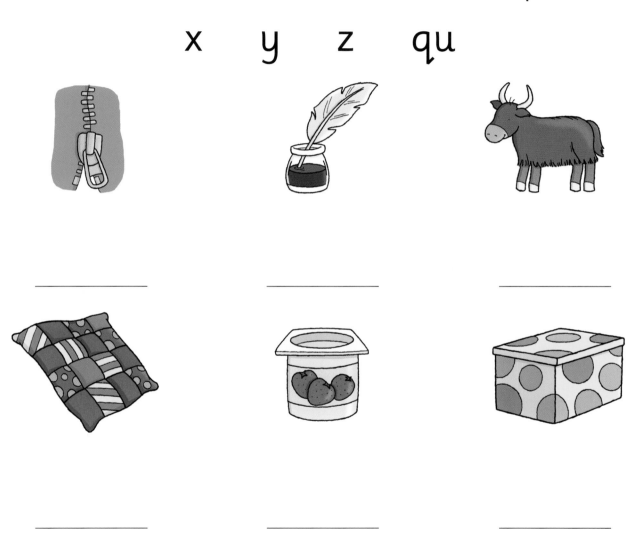

The words are: zip, quill, yak, quilt, yoghurt, box.

Say each word, then choose the correct letters for the start sound. Choose the end sound for the last three pictures.

ch   sh   th   ng

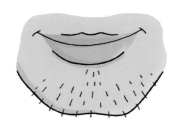  

The words are: chin, thin, sheep, teeth, moth, king.

Say the sounds, work out the word and point to the correct picture.

chip		
moth		
shop		
sing		

Say the word and write the correct letters for the start sound from the ones below. Write the end sound for the last picture.

ch sh th ng

_____

_____

_____

_____

_____

_____

The words are: chip, shop, ship, thin, chin, ring.

Say each word, then choose the correct letters for the vowel sound from the ones below.

ai   ee   ie   oa

The words are: nail, tie, goat, bee, toast, train.

Say the sounds, work out the word and point to the correct picture.

rail		
pie		
feet		
boat		

Say each word, then choose the correct letters for the vowel sound from the ones below.

short **oo**　　long **OO**　　**ue**　　**ar**

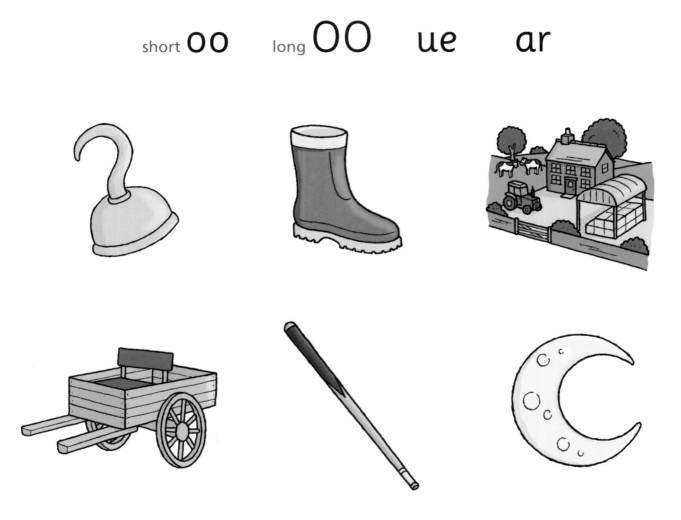

The words are: hook, boot, farm, cart, cue, moon.

Say the sounds, work out the word and point to the correct picture.

cue		
book		
park		
moon		

Say each word, then choose the correct letters for the sound from the ones below.

or   er   ou   oi

The words are: boil, fern, horn, mouth, corn, cloud.

Say the sounds, work out the word and point to the correct picture.

port		
number		
coin		
loud		

Say the sounds, work out the word and point to the correct picture.

tent		
belt		
lamp		
pond		

Say the sounds, work out the word and point to the correct picture.

flag		
drum		
crab		
pram		